MW00886089

Teacher Guide and Novel Unit for Pax

By:

John Pennington

Cover Image by: Pixabay.com

The lessons on demand series is designed to provide ready to use resources for novel study. In this book you will find key vocabulary, student organizer pages, and assessments. This guide is divided into two sections. Section one is the teacher section which consists of vocabulary and activities. Section two holds all of the student pages, including assessments and graphic organizers.

Now available! Student Workbooks!

Find them on Amazon.com

Other titles include...

The War That Saved My Life

Esperanza Rising

Walk Two Moons

The Giver

One Crazy Summer

The One and Only Ivan

Flora & Ulysses

Island of the Blue Dolphin

The Little Prince

The Lightning Thief

Where the Red Fern Grows

And more........

Section One

Teacher Pages

Vocabulary

Suggested Activities

Chapters 1-2 Vocabulary

Odors

Anxiety

Ruff

Marrow

Protection

Distraction

Affection

Fractured

Surreptitiously

Inseparable

Coyote

Chapters 1-2 Activities

Main Plot of Chapters

Peter drops off PAX on his way to live with his grandfather

Reading Check Question:

How does Peter get PAX to leave? Plays catch with the plastic army man

Blooms Higher Order Question:

Infer the meaning behind the opening quote "Just because it isn't happening here doesn't mean it isn't happening."

Evaluate the fairness of Peters father having Duke.

Suggested Activity Sheets (see Section Two):

Character Sketch—Peter, PAX, Father, Grandfather

Top Ten—List the top ten items in Peters backpack

Chapters 3-5 Vocabulary

Thermals

Carrion

Decay

Diesel

Culvert

Civilization

Reflection

Vixen

Submission

Exotic

Subdued

Chapters 3-5 Activities

Main Plot of Chapter

PAX is determined to wait for Peter by the road.

Peter stops to buy a flashlight.

PAX meets Bristle and Runt.

Reading Check Question:

Why is Bristle cautious of PAX? He smells like a human

Blooms Higher Order Question:

Critique Peters use of his money to buy a flashlight

Suggested Activity Sheets (see Section Two):

Character Sketch Bristle, Runt

Research—animals in captivity

Chapters 6-7 Vocabulary

Puffballs

Therapist

Piteously

Perpendicular

Denser

Twilight

Circumstances

Predators

Alpha

Comportment

Deception

Chapters 6-7 Activities

Main Plot of Chapter

Peter leaves town but breaks his bone tripping on a root.

PAX discusses with Gray the concept of human war-sickness.

Reading Check Question:

What happened to Peter after he got stuck in the swamp? Tripped and broke his bone,

What did PAX need but was not leaving the road for? Water

Blooms Higher Order Question:

Evaluate what actions humans take that Gray does not trust

Critique Peters decisions on how to find PAX

Research—therapist

Suggested Activity Sheets (see Section Two):

Character Sketch—Gray

Precognition sheet—what will happen next (Peter or PAX)

Chapter 8-9 Vocabulary

Scythes

Syllables

Accent

Nondisplaced

Fracture

Metatarsal

Hypothermia

Gable

Poultice

Arnica

Comfrey

Willow

Chapter 8-9 Activities

Main Plot of Chapter

Peter wakes up in Vola's barn. She helps him by building him crutches.

PAX and Gray go back to Bristle, Runt and Gray's mate to rest before taking the trip south.

Reading Check Question:

What did Peter take from Vola because he was afraid? Her knife

What was happening to Bristle when PAX and Gray show up? She was fighting off another fox

Blooms Higher Order Question:

Infer why Vola acts the way she does to Peter.

Suggested Activity Sheets (see Section Two):

Lost Scene—write a scene about the time Vola lost her leg

Character sketch—Vola

Research this - the bones of the body

Chapter 10-13 Vocabulary

Scowl

Vivid

Piteous

Sympathy

Consequential

Cinnamon

Electricity

Scarecrow

Companion

Outhouse

Prosthetic

Carrion

Chapter 10-13 Activities

Main Plot of Chapter

Peter goes back and gets help from Vola

Bristle tells PAX of how her family died

PAX is fed eggs by Runt

Reading Check Question:

Why does Bristle dislike the smell of Humans? They were responsible for killing her family

Why does Vola agree to help Peter? He believes it is something he has to do in his core

Blooms Higher Order Question:

Critique the statement about peace made my Peter and Vola. (chapter 12)

Suggested Activity Sheets (see Section Two):

Compare and contrast—how Peter and PAX are taken care of

Making Connections—to the concept of wild or tame

Chapter 14-15 Vocabulary

Phoenix

Myrrh

Philosophy

PTSD

Flanked

Divine

Instinct

Murder of crows

Chaos

Discord

Chapter 14-15 Activities

Main Plot of Chapter

Vola tells her story to Peter.

PAX and Gray travel together, PAX discovers Peters father.

Reading Check Question:

What about the phoenix story was Peter's mothers favorite part? Rising from its OWN ashes

Why was Gray having trouble traveling? He was bitten by another fox

Blooms Higher Order Question:

Produce you own philosophy bingo cards

Predict how Peters father will react to PAX if he sees him

Suggested Activity Sheets (see Section Two):

Create the Test—Create questions using chapters 1-15

Write a letter—write the letter Peter needs to write to his grandfather

Chapter 16-18 Vocabulary

Marionettes

Courage

Roc

Voles

Wrens

Tormented

Nourish

Bonanza

Chisel

Mallet

Chapter 16-18 Activities

Main Plot of Chapter

Vola shows Peter the puppets she made to tell the story of Sinbad

Gray is killed by a human explosion

Peter wants to learn how to carve PAX from wood

Reading Check Question:

Why does Vola want to tell the story of Sinbad? It meant something to the person she killed

How does Gray die? An explosion caused by the human war

Blooms Higher Order Question:

Compare how Peter remembers PAX to how he remembers his mother

Evaluate PAX's decisions

Suggested Activity Sheets (see Section Two):

Sequencing—(two sheets) One for Peter one for PAX for chapters 1-18

What would you do? - pick either Peter or PAX

Interpret this— "I saw the angel in the marble and carved until I set him free."

Chapter 19-22 Vocabulary

Trenches

Eddied

Buddhist

Nonduality

Inherited

Grenade

Unpredictable

Shelter

Technique

Camouflage

Protest

Protein

Chapter 19-22 Vocabulary

Main Plot of Chapter

PAX goes back to the field, Bristle and Runt follow, Runt is caught in an explosion. PAX realizes that Peter was false with him.

Peter performs a play for Vola, it is about her and not the one she expects.

Reading Check Question:

Who gets injured following PAX? Runt

Who is the play about that Peter performs? Vola

Blooms Higher Order Question:

Propose a meaning to peters play

Judge if Peter will eventually become war-sick

Suggested Activity Sheets (see Section Two):

Draw the scene—Peters play

Support this—Human, Tame or Wild

Do you Agree? Ch20 "Plenty hard. The plain truth can be the hardest thing to see when it's about yourself. If you don't want to know the truth, you'll do anything to disguise it."

Chapter 23-25 Vocabulary

Cached

Penance

Ti Poul

Perimeter

Juniper

Aggression

Primitive

Composure

Chapter 23-25 Activities

Main Plot of Chapter

PAX steals some food from the Humans, is caught, but Peter's father lets him escape

Vola puts Peter on the bus and agrees to Peters three conditions

PAX learns how to hunt, feels free

Reading Check Question:

What does PAX take from the humans? Peanut butter

What does Vola do with her marionettes? Donates them and her time to the library

Blooms Higher Order Question:

Decide what PAX will decide to do if he meets Peter again

Interpret Vola using the term family as Peter leaves

Suggested Activity Sheets (see Section Two):

Who, what, where, when, and how—questions for chapters 23-25

Write a letter—from the point of view of one of the students thanking Vola for her time teaching them

Chapter 26-28 Vocabulary

Barricade

Evacuated

Vacant

Abandoned

Murmurs

Meadow

Plateau

Gorge

Adrenaline

Absorbed

Main Plot of Chapter

Peter makes it back to where he left PAX

PAX knows that Peter is near

Peter continues to look for PAX

Reading Check Question:

Why does the guard let Peter cross? He also left a companion behind

What does Peter do to his leg? Cuts a piece off because he wants to know how it would feel

Blooms Higher Order Question:

Develop a statement about what the meaning of tame and wild

Conclude using text from the book if humans are tame or wild

Suggested Activity Sheets (see Section Two):

Precognition sheet—predict how the story will end for Peter or PAX

Interpret this! - And why didn't anyone count those things? "People should tell the truth about what war costs," Vola had said. Weren't those things the costs of war, too? Chapter 28

Chapter 29-34 Vocabulary

Vulnerable

Burrow

Taunt

Iridescent

Devastation

Defiance

Cordite

Loyalty

Chapter 29-34 Activities

Main Plot of Chapter

PAX, Bristle and Runt are attacked by Coyotes

Peter and PAX are reunited

Reading Check Question:

How many coyotes attack PAX and Bristle? Two

What does Peter decide to do when reunited with PAX? Thrown the army man

Blooms Higher Order Question:

Choose who PAX would stay with in the end and why

Evaluate how Peter has changed from the beginning

Suggested Activity Sheets (see Section Two):

Pyramid— use to rank the important concepts in the book from most important to least

Lost Scene—write the next scene of the book

Create the test—create test questions from chapter 15-34

Do you agree? - "Do you think anyone in the history of this world ever set out to fight for the wrong side?" Chapter 30

Section Two

Student Work Pages

Work Pages

Graphic Organizers

Assessments

Activity Descriptions

Advertisement—Select an item from the text and have the students use text clues to draw an advertisement about that item.

Chapter to Poem—Students select 20 words from the text to write a five line poem with 3 words on each line.

Character Sketch—Students complete the information about a character using text clues.

Comic Strip— Students will create a visual representation of the chapter in a series of drawings.

Compare and Contrast—Select two items to make relationship connections with text support.

Create the Test—have the students use the text to create appropriate test questions.

Draw the Scene—students use text clues to draw a visual representation of the chapter.

Interview— Students design questions you would ask a character in the book and then write that characters response.

Lost Scene—Students use text clues to decide what would happen after a certain place in the story.

Making Connections—students use the text to find two items that are connected and label what kind of relationship connects them.

Precognition Sheet—students envision a character, think about what will happen next, and then determine what the result of that would be.

Activity Descriptions

Pyramid—Students use the text to arrange a series of items in an hierarchy format.

Research Connection—Students use an outside source to learn more about a topic in the text.

Sequencing—students will arrange events in the text in order given a specific context.

Support This! - Students use text to support a specific idea or concept.

Travel Brochure—Students use information in the text to create an informational text about the location

Top Ten List—Students create a list of items ranked from 1 to 10 with a specific theme.

Vocabulary Box—Students explore certain vocabulary words used in the text.

What Would You Do? - Students compare how characters in the text would react and compare that with how they personally would react.

Who, What, When, Where, and How—Students create a series of questions that begin with the following words that are connected to the text.

Write a Letter—Students write a letter to a character in the text.

Activity Descriptions (for scripts and poems)

Add a Character—Students will add a character that does not appear in the scene and create dialog and responses from other characters.

Costume Design—Students will design costumes that are appropriate to the characters in the scene and explain why they chose the design.

Props Needed— Students will make a list of props they believe are needed and justify their choices with text.

Soundtrack! - Students will create a sound track they believe fits the play and justify each song choice.

Stage Directions— Students will decide how the characters should move on, around, or off stage.

Poetry Analysis—Students will determine the plot, theme, setting, subject, tone and important words and phrases.

Advertisement: Draw an advertisement for the book

NAME:

TEACHER:

Date:

Title:

_____ _____ _____

_____ _____ _____

_____ _____ _____

_____ _____ _____

_____ _____ _____

NAME:

Character Sketch

Name

Draw a picture

Personality/ Distinguishing marks

Connections to other characters

Important Actions

NAME:

Comic Strip

NAME:

TEACHER:

Date:

Compare and Contrast

Venn Diagram

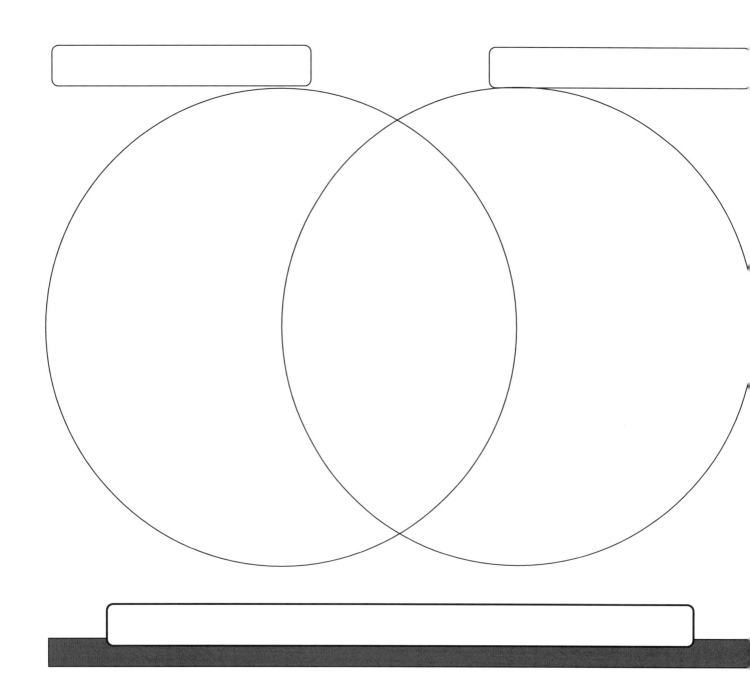

NAME:

TEACHER:

Date:

Create the Test

Question:

Answer:

Question:

Answer:

Question:

Answer:

Question:

Answer:

NAME:

TEACHER:

Date:

Draw the Scene: What five things have you included in the scene?

1   2   3

4   5

NAME:

TEACHER:

Date:

Interview: Who _____

Question:

Answer:

Question:

Answer:

Question:

Answer:

Question:

Answer:

Lost Scene: Write a scene that takes place between _____ and _____

NAME:

TEACHER:

Date:

Making Connections

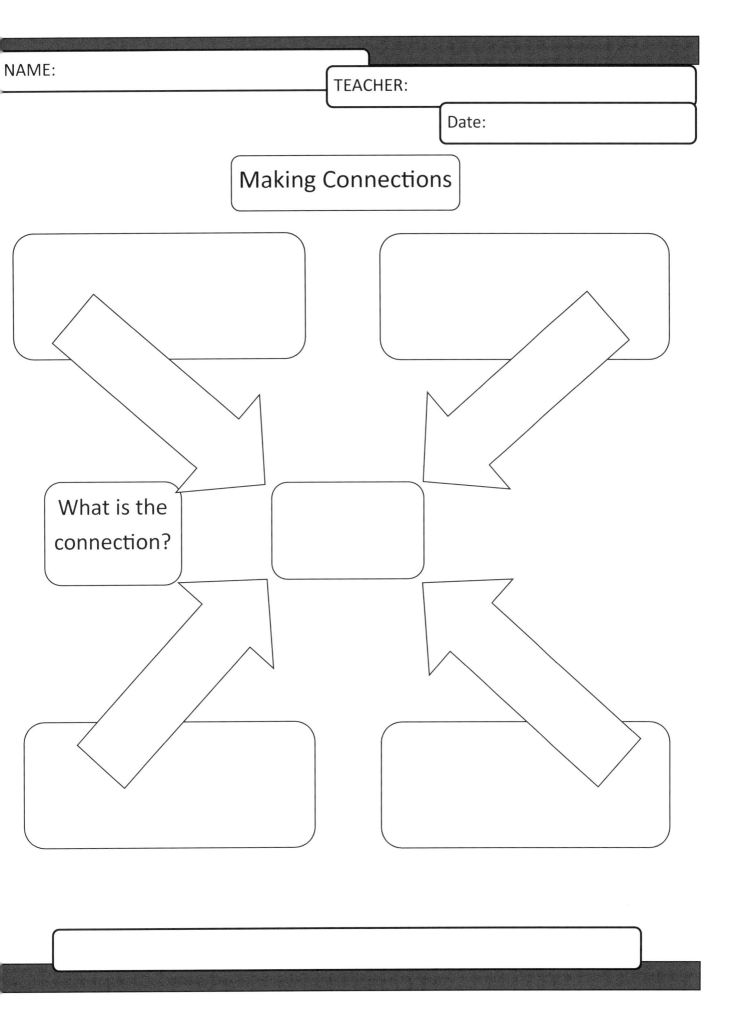

What is the connection?

NAME:

TEACHER:

Date:

Precognition Sheet

Who ?

What's going to happen?

What will be the result?

Who ?

What's going to happen?

What will be the result?

Who ?

What's going to happen?

What will be the result?

Who ?

What's going to happen?

What will be the result?

How many did you get correct?

NAME:

TEACHER:

Date:

Assignment: Pyramid

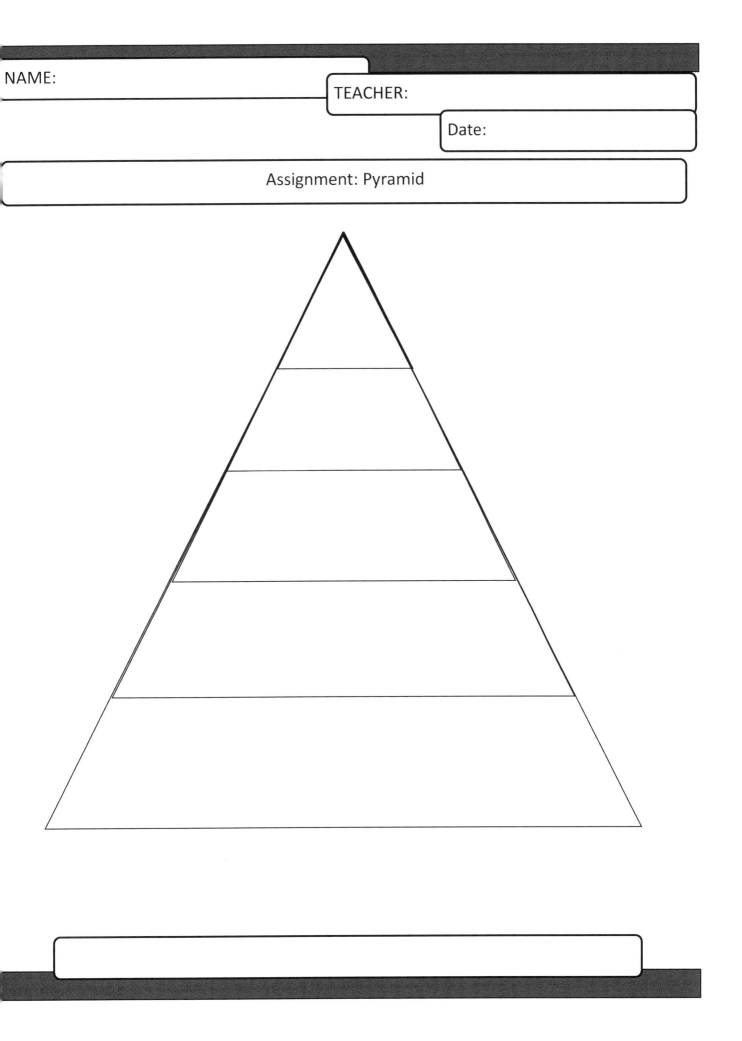

NAME:

TEACHER:

Date:

Research connections

Source (URL, Book, Magazine, Interview)

What am I researching?

Facts I found that could be useful or notes

1.

2.

3.

4.

5.

6.

NAME:

TEACHER:

Date:

1.

Sequencing
or timeline

2.

3.

4.

5.

NAME:

Support This!

Supporting text

What page?

Supporting text

What page?

Central idea or statement

Supporting text

What page?

Supporting text

What page?

Travel Brochure

Why should you visit?

What are you going to see?

Map

Special Events

Top Ten List

1.

2.

3.

4.

5.

6.

7.

8.

9.

10.

NAME:

TEACHER:

Date:

Vocabulary Box

Definition:

Draw:

Word:

Related words:

Use in a sentence:

Definition:

Draw:

Word:

Related words:

Use in a sentence:

NAME:

TEACHER:

Date:

What would you do?

Character: _____

What did they do?

Example from text:

What would you do?

Why would that be better?

Character: _____

What did they do?

Example from text:

What would you do?

Why would that be better?

Character: _____

What did they do?

Example from text:

What would you do?

Why would that be better?

NAME:

TEACHER:

Date:

Who, What, When, Where, and How

Who

What

Where

When

How

Write a letter

To:

From:

NAME:

TEACHER:

Date:

Assignment:

Add a Character

Who is the new character?

What reason does the new character have for being there?

Write a dialog between the new character and characters currently in the scene.

You dialog must be 6 lines or more, and can occur in the beginning, middle or end of the scene.

NAME:

TEACHER:

Date:

Costume Design

Draw a costume for one the characters in the scene.

Why do you believe this character should have a costume like this?

NAME:

TEACHER:

Date:

Props Needed

Prop:

What text from the scene supports this?

Prop:

What text from the scene supports this?

Prop:

What text from the scene supports this?

NAME:

TEACHER:

Date:

Soundtrack!

Song:

Why should this song be used?

Song:

Why should this song be used?

Song:

Why should this song be used?

Stage Directions

List who is moving, how they are moving and use text from the dialog to determine when they move.

Who:

How:

When:

Who:

How:

When:

Who:

How:

When:

NAME:

TEACHER:

Poetry Analysis

Date:

Name of Poem:

Subject:

Text Support:

Plot:

Text Support:

Theme:

Text Support:

Setting:

Text Support:

Tone:

Text Support:

Important Words and Phrases:

Why are these words and phrases important:

Made in the USA
Coppell, TX
08 August 2020

32762058R00033